THE GIRL WHO CLIMBED MOUNTAINS

This book belongs to

Read more in the Dreamers series by Lavanya Karthik

dreamerS

THE GIRL WHO CLIMBED MOUNTAINS

BACHENDRI PAL

Written and illustrated by
LAVANYA KARTHIK

duckbill

An imprint of Penguin Random House

For you and the mountains you will climb

DUCKBILL BOOKS

USA | Canada | UK | Ireland | Australia
New Zealand | India | South Africa | China

Duckbill Books is part of the Penguin Random House group of companies
whose addresses can be found at global.penguinrandomhouse.com

Published by Penguin Random House India Pvt. Ltd
4th Floor, Capital Tower 1, MG Road,
Gurugram 122 002, Haryana, India

Penguin
Random House
India

First published in Duckbill Books by
Penguin Random House India 2022

Text and illustrations copyright © Lavanya Karthik 2022

10 9 8 7 6 5 4 3 2

This book is, as the author claims, a work of 'faction' and, while fixed both historically
and chronologically, remains fiction, based on fact, embroidered and distorted in order
to project the character herein. All names, save where obviously genuine, are fictitious
and any resemblance to persons living or dead is wholly coincidental.

ISBN 9780143457657

Typeset in Georgia by DiTech Publishing Services Pvt. Ltd
Printed at Aarvee Promotions, India

www.penguin.co.in

Before Bachendri Pal created history as the first Indian woman to climb Mt. Everest, she was a girl called Bachni, in the hills of Garhwal. Born to a family of sheep herders, Bachni was a small girl with big dreams.

This is her story.

High up in Harsil Valley, in the shadow of the Himalayas, our tiny village was our world.

And the mountains?

They were our gods.
And when the gods call, you listen.

There were ten of us that lazy Sunday morning, free from school work for the day. 'A picnic!' said Bachan, my older brother, and we all agreed.

But where would we go?

As one, our eyes turned towards
the great mountain, looming over
the valley.

'Girls can't climb, Bachni!' Bachan teased.

'We'll prove you wrong!' I laughed.

'Mother says the mountain is a sleeping god!' Nayani, my best friend, said.

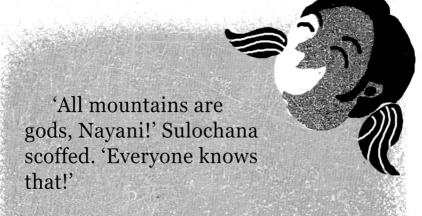

'All mountains are gods, Nayani!' Sulochana scoffed. 'Everyone knows that!'

'Father says there are demons up there, too!' Alam's eyes were wide.

'Race you!' I shouted.
And we were off.

We laughed and sang as we climbed. We ran through the trees, jumped over rocks, and raced to see who would reach the snowline first.

Late in the afternoon, we
reached the top of the mountain.

Everything seemed so small, so far away—our village, our families, even our troubles.

Baba said I was naughty and restless. Aamah said I wasted my time dreaming, that I ought to be more like my sisters, gentle and skilled at housework. And Bachan—he thought girls couldn't climb!

Held up in the palm of the mountain god, I felt my dreams grow as big as the sky.

On our journey home, the demons found us.

THIRST was first.

His dry, bony fingers closed in around our throats. We searched in vain for a stream, then struggled to swallow snow.

COLD followed, freezing our bones through the thin summer clothes we wore. We huddled together, our teeth chattering, and struggled to keep warm.

FEAR reared his ugly head as the slopes grew slippery with ice. It was too dangerous for us to walk on.

By the light of a fire we built
from twigs, we fought those demons
together.

'The mountain is angry!' Sulochana trembled. 'We never should have come!'

'The demons will get us!' Alam stuttered. 'They're punishing us for climbing the mountain!'

THIRST grew stronger.
FEAR grew bolder.
COLD tore at us with rage.

𝕾𝖎𝖈𝖐𝖓𝖊𝖘𝖘 joined her friends, leaving us giddy, aching and ill.

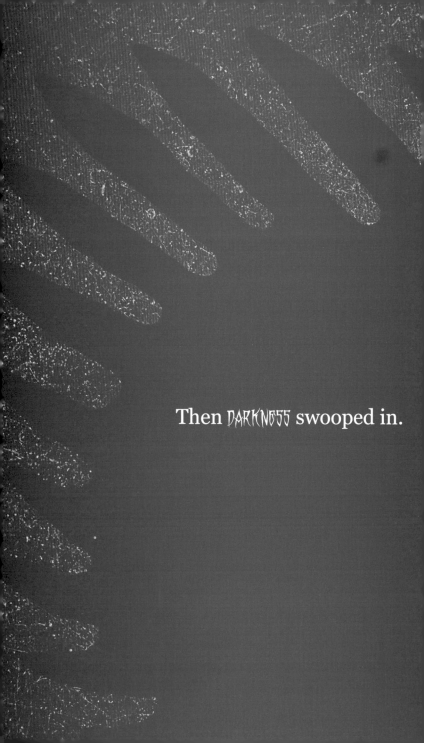

Then DARKNESS swooped in.

All night those demons taunted us.
All night my friends and I fought back.
Until . . .

The first rays of the sun reached
down to warm us.

Light flooded in.

The demons faded away.

How big everything seemed now,
as we raced down to the valley—
the comfort of home, the embrace of
family, the promise of another day.

And after my night with
the demons, my own heart.

At the feet of the mountain god, I felt my dreams soar up towards the sky.

The demons weren't punishment, they were a test. And the song in my heart a gift for answering the mountain's call.

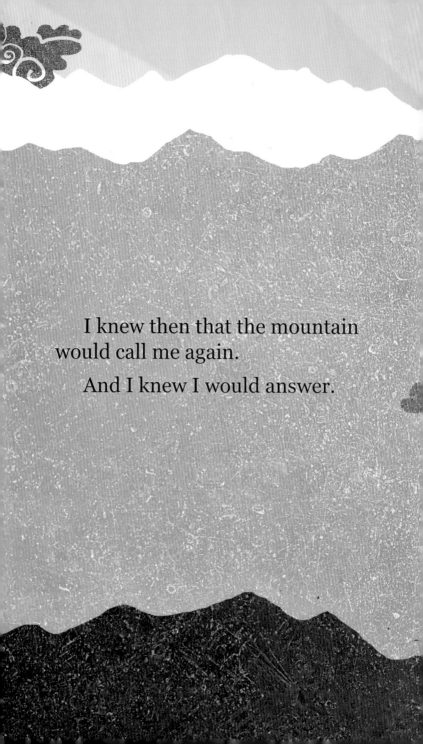

I knew then that the mountain would call me again.

And I knew I would answer.

Bachni and her friends would learn that they had climbed nearly 4000 metres. The nausea and headaches they felt was the result of altitude sickness, brought on by lower oxygen levels at that height.

Bachendri Pal (b. 24 May 1954) was part of an Indian expedition that successfully reached the summit of Mt. Everest in 1984. Braving icy winds and even an avalanche that buried her camp, she became the first Indian woman

to climb the Everest, just one day before her thirtieth birthday. She went on to lead many expeditions in the Himalayas, inspiring scores of women to follow in her footsteps. As director of the Tata Steel Adventure Foundation in Jamshedpur, she continues to spread her love for mountains and the great outdoors.

She has won many prestigious awards for mountaineering, including the Padma Shri, the Padma Bhushan and the Arjuna Award.

The illustrations in this book are inspired by thangka art.

The author wishes to thank Ms Bachendri Pal for her invaluable help in the making of this book.

Lavanya Karthik is an author and illustrator by day, a cookie monster by teatime, and fast asleep by nine at night. She lives in Mumbai where she eats a lot of chocolate and takes a lot of naps.